Knots, Splices and Rope Work

An Illustrated Handbook

Knots, Splices and Rope Work
An Illustrated Handbook

A. Hyatt Verrill

Dover Publications, Inc.
Mineola, New York

Bibliographical Note

This Dover edition, first published in 2006, is an unabridged republication of the 1917 (third revised) edition of the work originally published in 1912 by the Norman W. Henley Publishing Co., New York, under the title *Knots, Splices and Rope Work: A Practical Treatise.*

Library of Congress Cataloging-in-Publication Data

Verrill, A. Hyatt (Alpheus Hyatt), 1871–1954.
  Knots, splices, and rope work : an illustrated handbook / A. Hyatt Verrill.
      p. cm.
  Reprint. Originally published: New York : Norman W. Henley Pub. Co., 1917.
  Includes index.
  ISBN 0-486-44789-8 (pbk.)
  1. Knots and splices. I. Title.

VM533.V5 2006
623.88'82—dc22

2006040314

Manufactured in the United States of America
Dover Publications, Inc., 31 East 2nd Street, Mineola, N.Y. 11501

CONTENTS

6   CONTENTS

CHAPTER IV

CHAPTER V

CHAPTER VI

CHAPTER VII

INTRODUCTION

THE history of ropes and knots is so dim and ancient that really little is known of their origin. That earliest man used cordage of some kind and by his ingenuity succeeded in tying the material together, is indisputable, for the most ancient carvings and decorations of prehistoric man show knots in several forms. Doubtless the trailing vines and plants first suggested ropes to human beings; and it is quite probable that these same vines, in their various twistings and twinings, gave man his first idea of knots.

Since the earliest times knots have been everywhere interwoven with human affairs; jugglers have used them in their tricks; they have become almost a part of many occupations and trades, while in song and story they have become the symbol of steadfastness and strength.

Few realize the importance that knots and cordage have played in the world's history, but if it had not been for these simple and every-day things, which as a rule are given far too little consideration, the human race could never have developed beyond savages. Indeed, I am not sure but it would be safe to state that the real difference between civilized and savage man consists largely in the knowledge of knots and rope work. No cloth could be woven, no net or seine knitted, no bow strung and no craft sailed on lake or sea without numerous knots and proper lines or ropes; and Columbus himself would have been far more handicapped without knots than without a compass.

History abounds with mention of knots, and in the eighth book of "Odyssey" Ulysses is represented as securing various articles of raiment by a rope fastened in a "knot closed with Circean art"; and as further proof of the prominence the ancients gave to knots the famous Gordian Knot may be mentioned. Probably no one will ever learn just how this fabulous knot was tied, and like many modern knots it was doubtless far easier for Alexander to cut it than to untie it.

The old sorcerers used knots in various ways, and the witches of Lapland sold sailors so-called "Wind Knots," which were untied by the sailors when they desired a particular wind. Even modern conjurors and wizards use knots extensively in their exhibitions and upon the accuracy and manner in which their knots are tied depends the success of their tricks.

In heraldry many knots have been used as symbols and badges and many old Coats of Arms bear intricate and handsome knots, or entwined ropes, emblazoned upon them.

As to the utility of knots and rope work there can be no question. A little knowledge of knots has saved many a life in storm and wreck, and if every one knew how to quickly and securely tie a knot there would be far fewer casualities in hotel and similar fires. In a thousand ways and times a knowledge of rope and knots is useful and many times necessary. Many an accident has occurred through a knot or splice being improperly formed, and even in tying an ordinary bundle or "roping" a trunk or box few people tie a knot that is secure and yet readily undone and quickly made. In a life of travel and adventure in out-of-the-way places, in yachting or boating, in hunting or fishing, and even in motoring, to command a number of good knots and splices is to make life safer, easier, and more enjoyable, aside from the real pleasure one may find in learning the interesting art of knot-tying.

Through countless ages the various forms of knots and fastenings for rope, cable, or cord have been developed; the best kinds being steadily improved and handed down from generation to generation, while the poor or inferior fastenings have been discarded by those whose callings required the use of cordage.

Gradually, too, each profession or trade has adopted the knots best suited to its requirements, and thus we find the Sailor's Knot; the Weaver's Knot; Fishermen's knots; Builders' knots; Butchers' knots; and many others which have taken their names from the use to which they are especially adapted.

In addition to these useful knots, there

are many kinds of ornamental or fancy knots used in ornamenting the ends of ropes, decorating shrouds of vessels, railings, and similar objects; while certain braids or plaits, formed by a series of knots, are widely used aboard ship and on land.

In many cases ropes or cable must be joined in such a way that they present a smooth and even surface and for such purposes splices are used, while knots used merely as temporary fastenings and which must be readily and quickly tied and untied are commonly known as "bends" or "hitches." Oddly enough, it is far easier to tie a poor knot than a good one, and in ninety-nine cases out of a hundred the tyro, when attempting to join two ropes together, will tie either a "slippery" or a "jamming" knot and will seldom succeed in making a recognized and "ship-shape" knot of any sort.

The number of knots, ties, bends, hitches, splices, and shortenings in use is almost unlimited and they are most confusing and bewildering to the uninitiated. The most useful and ornamental, as well as the most reliable, are comparatively few in number, and in reality each knot learned leads readily to another; in the following pages I have endeavored to describe them in such a manner that their construction may be readily understood and mastered.

THE AUTHOR.

April, 1912.

KNOTS, SPLICES AND ROPE WORK

CHAPTER I

CORDAGE

Before taking up the matter of knots and splices in detail it may be well to give attention to cordage in general. Cordage, in its broadest sense, includes all forms and kinds of rope, string, twine, cable, etc., formed of braided or twisted strands. In making a rope or line the fibres (A, Fig. 1) of hemp, jute, cotton, or other material are loosely twisted together to form what is technically known as a "yarn" (B, Fig. 1). When two or more yarns are twisted together they form a "strand" (C, Fig. 1). Three or more strands form a rope (D, Fig. 1), and three ropes form a cable (E, Fig. 1). To form a strand the yarns are twisted together in the opposite direction from that in which the original fibres were twisted; to form a rope the strands are twisted in the opposite direction from the yarns of the strands, and to form a cable each rope is twisted opposite from the twist of the strands. In this way the natural tendency for each yarn, strand, or rope to untwist serves to bind or hold the whole firmly together (Fig. 1).

Rope is usually three-stranded and the

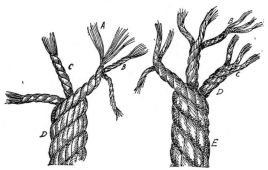

FIG. 1.—Construction of rope.

strands turn from left to right or "with the sun," while cable is left-handed or twisted "against the sun" (E, Fig. 1). Certain ropes, such as "bolt-rope" and most cables, are laid around a "core" (F, Fig. 2) or central strand and in many cases are four-stranded (Fig. 2).

The strength of a rope depends largely upon the strength and length of the fibres from which it is made, but the amount each

yarn and strand is twisted, as well as the
method used in bleaching or preparing the
fibres, has much to do with the strength of
the finished line.

Roughly, the strength of ropes may be
calculated by multiplying the circumference

FIG. 2.—Bolt-rope.

of the rope in inches by itself and the fifth
part of the product will be the number of
tons the rope will sustain. For example,
if the rope is 5 inches in circumference,
$5 \times 5 = 25$, one-fifth of which is 5, the
number of tons that can safely be carried
on a 5-inch rope. To ascertain the weight
of ordinary "right hand" rope, multiply
the circumference in inches by itself and
multiply the result by the length of rope in
fathoms and divide the product by 3.75.

For example, to find the weight of a 5-inch rope, 50 fathoms in length: $5 \times 5 = 25$; $25 \times 50 = 1,250$; $1,250 \div 3.75 = 333\frac{1}{3}$ lbs. These figures apply to Manila or hemp rope, which is the kind commonly used, but jute, sisal-flax, grass, and silk are also used considerably. Cotton rope is seldom used save for small hand-lines, clothes-lines, twine, etc., while wire rope is largely used nowadays for rigging vessels, derricks, winches, etc., but as splicing wire rope is different from the method employed in fibre rope, and as knots have no place in wire rigging, we will not consider it.

CHAPTER II

SIMPLE KNOTS AND BENDS

For convenience in handling rope and learning the various knots, ties, and bends, we use the terms "standing part," "bight," and "end" (Fig. 3). The *Standing Part* is the principal portion or longest part of the rope; the *Bight* is the part curved or bent while working or handling; while the *End* is that part used in forming the knot or hitch. Before commencing work the loose ends or strands of a rope should be "whipped" or "seized" to prevent the rope from unravelling; and although an expert can readily tie almost any knot, make a splice, or in fact do pretty nearly anything with a loose-ended rope, yet it is a wise plan to invariably whip the end of every rope, cable, or hawser to be handled, while a marline-spike, fid, or pointed stick will also prove of great help in working rope.

To whip or seize a rope-end, take a piece of twine or string and lay it on the rope an

inch or two from the end, pass the twine
several times around the rope, keeping
the ends of the twine under the first few

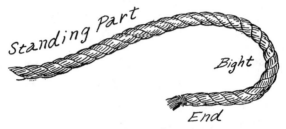

FIG. 3.—Parts of rope.

turns to hold it in place; then make a large
loop with the free end of twine; bring it
back to the rope and continue winding

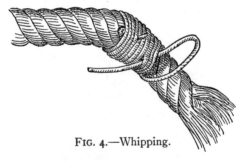

FIG. 4.—Whipping.

for three or four turns around both rope
and end of twine; and then finish by drawing the loop tight by pulling on the free
end (Fig. 4).

All knots are begun by "loops" or rings commonly known to mariners as "Cuckolds' Necks" (Fig. 5). These may be either over-

FIG. 5.—Cuckolds' necks.

hand or underhand, and when a seizing or fastening of twine is placed around the two parts where they cross a useful rope ring

FIG. 6.—Clinch.

known as a "clinch" is formed (Fig. 6). If the loose end of the rope is passed over the standing part and through the "cuck-

old's neck," the simplest of all knots, known
as the "Overhand Knot," is made (Fig. 7).
This drawn tight appears as in Fig. 8, and
while so simple this knot is important, as it

FIG. 7   FIG. 8
FIGS. 7 and 8.—Overhand knots.

is frequently used in fastening the ends of
yarns and strands in splicing, whipping, and
seizing. The "Figure-Eight Knot" is almost as simple as the overhand and is
plainly shown in Figs. 9 and 10. Only a

FIG. 9   FIG. 10
FIGS. 9 and 10.—Figure-eight knots.

step beyond the figure-eight and the overhand knots are the "Square" and "Reefing"
knots (Figs. 11 and 12). The square knot
is probably the most useful and widely used
of any common knot and is the best all-

around knot known. It is very strong, never slips or becomes jammed, and is readily untied. To make a square knot, take the ends of the rope and pass the left

Fig. 11   Fig. 12
Figs. 11 and 12.—Square knots.

end over and under the right end, then the right over and under the left. If you once learn the simple formula of "Left over," "Right over," you will never make a mis-

Fig. 13.—Granny knot.

take and form the despised "Granny," a most useless, bothersome, and deceptive makeshift for any purpose (Fig. 13). The true "Reef Knot" is merely the square knot with the bight of the left or right end used instead of the end itself.   This enables the knot to be "cast off" more readi y than the regular square knot (*A*, Fig. 12).   Neither square nor reef knots, however, are reliable

FIG. 14.—Slipped square knot.

when tying two ropes of unequal size together, for under such conditions they will frequently slip and appear as in Fig. 14, and sooner or later will pull apart.   To prevent this the ends may be tied or seized as

FIG. 15.—Square knot with ends seized.

shown in Fig. 15.   A better way to join two ropes of unequal diameter is to use the "Open-hand Knot."   This knot is shown in Fig. 16, and is very quickly and easily made; it never slips or gives, but is rather large and clumsy, and if too great a strain is put on the rope it is more likely to break at the knot than at any other spot. The "Fisherman's Knot," shown in Fig. 17, is a good knot and is formed by two simple overhand knots slipped over each rope,

FIG. 16.—Open-hand knots.

and when drawn taut appears as in Fig. 18. This is an important and valuable knot for anglers, as the two lines may be drawn apart by taking hold of the ends, A, B, and a third line for a sinker, or extra hook, may be inserted between them. In joining gut lines the knot should be left slightly open and the space between wrapped with silk. This is probably the strongest known method of fastening fine lines.

FIG. 17.—Fisherman's knot (making).

FIG. 18.—Fisherman's knot (finished).

The "Ordinary Knot," for fastening heavy ropes, is shown in Fig. 19. It is made by forming a simple knot and then

FIG. 19.—Ordinary knot (finished).

interlacing the other rope or "following around," as shown in Fig. 20. This knot is very strong, will not slip, is easy to make, and does not strain the fibres of the rope. Moreover, ropes joined with this knot will pay out, or hang, in a straight line. By whipping the ends to the standing parts it

FIG. 20.—Ordinary knot (tying).

becomes a neat and handsome knot (Fig. 21). The "Weaver's Knot" (Fig. 22) is more useful in joining small lines, or twine, than for rope, and for thread it is without

FIG. 21.—Ordinary knot (seized).

doubt the best knot known. The ends are crossed as in Fig. 23. The end *A* is then looped back over the end *B*, and the end *B* is slipped through loop *C* and drawn tight.

Another useful and handsome knot is illustrated in Fig. 24. This is a variation of the figure-eight knot, already described, and is used where there is too much rope,

FIG. 22.—Weaver's knot (complete).

or where a simple knot is desired to prevent the rope running through an eye, ring, or

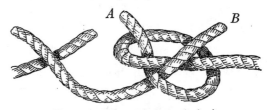

FIG. 23.—Weaver's knot (tying).

tackle-block. It is made by forming a regular figure eight and then "following

FIG. 24.—Double figure-eight knot (complete).

round" with the other rope as in Fig. 25. It is then drawn taut and the ends seized to the standing part if desired.

Sometimes we have occasion to join two heavy or stiff ropes or hawsers, and for this purpose the "Garrick Bend" (Fig. 26) is

FIG. 25.—Double figure-eight knot (tying).

preeminently the best of all knots. To make this knot, form a bight by laying

FIG. 26.—Garrick bend (finished).

the end of a rope on top of and across the standing part. Next take the end of the other rope and pass it through this bight,

first down, then up, over the cross and down
through the bight again, so that it comes
out on the opposite side from the other end,
thus bringing one end on top and the other

FIG. 27.—Garrick bend (tying).

below, as illustrated in Fig. 27.   If the lines
are very stiff or heavy the knot may be
secured by seizing the ends to the standing

FIG. 28.—Simple hitch (hawser).

parts.   A much simpler and a far poorer
knot is sometimes used in fastening two
heavy ropes together.   This is a simple
hitch within a loop, as illustrated in Fig.

28, but while it has the advantage of being quickly and easily tied it is so inferior to the Garrick bend that I advise all to adopt the latter in its place.

When two heavy lines are to be fastened for any considerable time, a good method

Fig. 29.—Half-hitch and seizing.

is to use the "Half-hitch and Seizing," shown in Fig. 29. This is a secure and easy method of fastening ropes together and it allows the rope to be handled more easily, and to pass around a winch or to be coiled much more readily, than when other knots are used.

CHAPTER III

Ties and Hitches

All the knots I have so far described are used mainly for fastening the two ends of a rope, or of two ropes, together. Of quite a different class are the knots used in making a rope fast to a stationary or solid object, and are known as "hitches" or "ties."

One of the easiest of this class to make and one which is very useful in fastening a boat or other object where it may be necessary to release it quickly is the "Lark's Head" (Fig. 30). To make this tie, pass a bight of your rope through the ring, or other object, to which you are making fast and then pass a marline-spike, a billet of wood, or any similar object through the sides of the bight and under or behind the standing part, as shown in A, Fig. 30. The end of the rope may then be laid over and under the standing part and back over itself. This knot may be instantly released

by merely pulling out the toggle. Almost
as quickly made and unfastened is the
"Slippery Hitch" (Fig. 32). To make this,
run the end of the rope through the ring
or eye to which it is being fastened, then
back over the standing part and pull a loop,

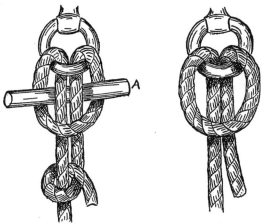

FIG. 30.—Lark's head with toggle (A). FIG. 31.—Lark's head with toggle (A) withdrawn.

or bight, back through the "cuckold's neck"
thus formed (Fig. 33). To untie, merely
pull on the free end. Two half-hitches,
either around a post or timber or around
the standing part of the rope, make an ideal
and quickly tied fastening (Figs. 34 and
35). To make these, pass the end around

the post, ring, or other object, then over
and around the standing part between the
post and itself, then under and around the

FIG. 32.—Slippery hitch
(complete).

FIG. 33.—Slippery hitch
(tying).

standing part and between its own loop and
the first one formed. After a little practice
you can tie this knot almost instantly and
by merely throwing a couple of turns
around a post, two half-hitches may be
formed instantly. This knot will hold
forever without loosening, and even on a
smooth, round stick or spar it will stand
an enormous strain without slipping. A
more secure knot for this same purpose is
the "Clove Hitch" (Fig. 36), sometimes

known as the "Builders' Hitch." To make
this, pass the end of rope around the spar
or timber, then over itself; over and
around the spar, and pass the end under
itself and between rope and spar, as shown
in the illustration. The Clove hitch with
ends knotted becomes the "Gunners' Knot"

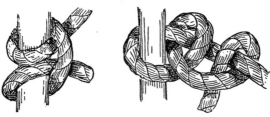

Fig. 34.   Fig. 35.
FIGS. 34 and 35.—Half-hitches.

(Fig. 37). These are among the most valuable and important of knots and are useful
in a thousand and one places. The Clove
hitch will hold fast on a smooth timber and
is used extensively by builders for fastening
the stageing to the upright posts. It is
also useful in making a tow-line fast to a
wet spar, or timber, and even on a slimy
and slippery spile it will seldom slip. For
this purpose the "Timber Hitch" (Fig. 32)
is even better than the Clove hitch. It is

easily made by passing the end of a rope around the spar or log, round the standing part of the rope and then twist it three or more times around, under and over itself.

FIG. 36 *A*.—Clove hitch or builder's hitch (tying).

FIG. 36 *B*.—Clove hitch (complete).

If you wish this still more secure, a single half-hitch may be taken with the line a couple of feet further along the spar (Fig. 39).

It is remarkable what power to grip a twisted rope has, and the "Twist Knots" shown in Figs. 40 and 41 illustrate two

FIG. 37.—Gunner's knot.

ways of making fast which are really not knots at all but merely twists. These may be finished by a simple knot, or a bow-knot,

FIG. 38.—Timber hitch.

as shown in Fig. 42, but they are likely to jam under great pressure and are mainly useful in tying packages, or bundles, with small cord, where the line must be held taut until the knot is completed.   This principle of fastening by twisted rope is also utilized

FIG. 39.—Timber hitch and half-hitch.

in the "Catspaw" (Fig. 43), a most useful knot or "hitch" for hoisting with a hook.

FIGS. 40 and 41.—"Twists."

To make this, pass the bight of your rope over the end and standing part, then, with a bight in each hand, take three twists from you, then bring the two bights side by side and throw over the hook (Fig. 44).

The "Blackwall Hitch" (Fig. 45) is still

FIG. 42.—Twist with bow.

simpler and easier to make and merely consists of a loop, or cuckold's neck, with the end of rope passed underneath the standing

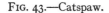

FIG. 43.—Catspaw.　　　FIG. 44.—Catspaw (tying).

part and across the hook so that as soon as pressure is exerted the standing part bears on the end and jams it against the hook.

FIG. 45.—Blackwall hitch.

The "Chain Hitch" (Fig. 46) is a very strong method of fastening a line to a timber, or large rope, where one has a rope of sufficient length, and is used frequently

FIG. 46.—Chain hitch.

to help haul in a large rope or for similar purposes. It consists simply of a number of half-hitches taken at intervals around the object and is sometimes used with a lever or handspike, as shown in Fig. 47. The "Rolling Hitch" is a modified Clove hitch and is shown in Fig. 48. The

FIG. 47.—Chain hitch with bar.

"Magnus Hitch" (Fig. 49) is a method frequently used on shipboard for holding spars; and the "Studding-sail Bend" (Fig. 50) is also used for this purpose. Occasions

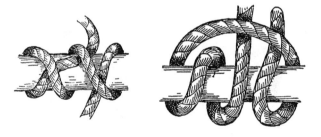

FIG. 48.—Rolling hitch.   FIG. 49.—Magnus hitch.

sometimes arise where a tackle, hook, ring, or another rope must be fastened to a beam by the same rope being used, and in such cases the "Roband Hitch" (Fig. 51) comes in very handy.   These are all so simple and easily understood from the figures that no

FIG. 50.—Studding-sail bend.

explanation is necessary.   Almost as simple are the "Midshipman's Hitch" (Fig. 52), the "Fisherman's Hitch" (Fig. 53), and the

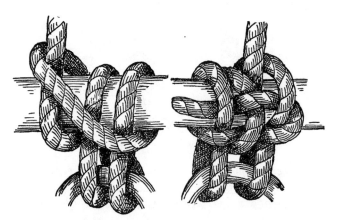

FIG. 51 *A*.—Roband hitch (front).

FIG. 51 *B*.—Roband hitch (back).

"Gaff Topsail Halyard Bend" (Fig. 54). The midshipman's hitch is made by taking a half-hitch around the standing part and a round turn twice around above it. The

FIG. 52.—Midshipman's hitch.

fisherman's hitch is particularly useful in making fast large hawsers; with the end of a rope take two turns around a spar, or through a ring; take a half-hitch around the standing part and under all the turns; then a half-hitch round the standing part only and if desired seize the end to standing

FIG. 53.—Fisherman's hitch.

part. The gaff-topsail bend is formed by passing two turns around the yard and

FIG. 54.—Gaff-topsail halyard bend.

coming up on a third turn over both the first two turns; over its own part and one turn; then stick the end under the first turn.

CHAPTER IV

Nooses, Loops and Mooring Knots

Nothing is more interesting to a landsman than the manner in which a sailor handles huge, dripping hawsers or cables and with a few deft turns makes then fast to a pier-head or spile, in such a way that the ship's winches, warping the huge structure o or from the dock, do not cause the slightest give or slip to the rope and yet, a moment later, with a few quick motions, the line is cast off, tightened up anew, or paid out as required   Clove hitches, used as illustrated in Fig. 55, and known as the "Waterman's Knot," are often used, with a man holding the free end, for in this way a slight pull holds the knot fast, while a little slack gives the knot a chance to slip without giving way entirely and without exerting any appreciable pull on the man holding the end.

"Larks' Heads" are also used in conjunction with a running noose, as shown in Fig.

56, while a few turns under and over and around a cleat, or about two spiles, is a

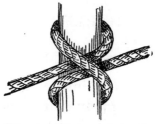

FIG. 55.—Waterman's knot.

method easily understood and universally used by sailors (Fig. 57). The sailor's knot

FIG. 56.—Larks' heads and running noose.

par excellence, however, is the "Bow-line" (Fig. 58), and wherever we find sailors, or

seamen, we will find this knot in one or
another of its various forms. When you
can readily and surely tie this knot every
time, you may feel yourself on the road to
"Marline-spike Seamanship," for it is a true

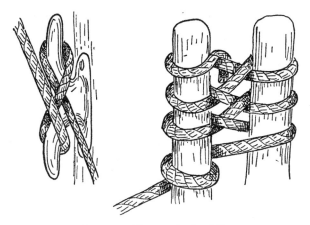

FIG. 57.—Cleat and wharf ties.

sailor's knot and never slips, jams, or fails;
is easily and quickly untied, and is useful
in a hundred places around boats or in fact
in any walk of life. The knot in its various
stages is well shown in Fig. 59 and by
following these illustrations you will under-
stand it much better than by a description
alone. In *A* the rope is shown with a bight
or cuckold's neck formed with the end over

the standing part. Pass *A* back through the bight, under, then over, then under, as shown in *B*, then over and down through the bight, as shown in *C* and *D*, and draw

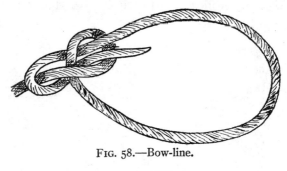

FIG. 58.—Bow-line.

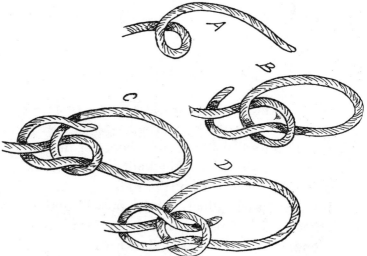

FIG. 59.—Tying bow-line.

taut, as in *E*. The "Bow-line on a Bight"
(Fig 60) is just as easily made and is very
useful in slinging casks or barrels and in
forming a seat for men to be lowered over
cliffs, or buildings, or to be hoisted aloft

FIG. 60.—Bow-line on bight.   FIG. 61.—Running bow-line.

aboard ship for painting, cleaning, or rigging.
A "Running Bow-line" (Fig. 61) is merely a
bow-line with the end passed through the
loop, thus forming a slip knot. Other
"Loops" are made as shown in F gs. 62–65,
but none of these are as safe, sure, and useful
as the bow-line. One of these knots, known
as the "Tomfool Knot" (Fig. 66), is used as

handcuffs and has become quite famous,
owing to its having baffled a number of
"Handcuff Kings" and other performers

FIG. 62.—Loop knot.

FIG. 63.—Loop knot.

FIG. 64.—Loop knot.

FIG. 65.—Loop knot.

who readily escaped from common knots and
manacles.   It is made like the running knot
(Fig. 62), and the firm end is then passed

through the open, simple knot so as to form a double loop or bow.   If the hands or wrists are placed within these loops and

FIG. 66.—Tomfool knot.

the latter drawn taut, and the loose ends tied firmly around the central part, a pair of wonderfully secure handcuffs results.

CHAPTER V

SHORTENINGS, GROMMETS, AND SELVAGEES

In many cases a rope may prove too long for our use or the free ends may be awkward, or in the way. At such times a knowledge of "shortenings" is valuable. There are quite a variety of these useful knots, nearly all of which are rather handsome and ornamental, in fact a number of them are in constant use aboard ship merely for ornament.

The simplest form of shortening, shown in Fig. 67, is a variation of the common and simple overhand knot already described and illustrated. These knots are formed by passing the end of a rope twice or more times through the loop of the simple knot and then drawing it tight (Fig. 68). They are known as "Double," "Treble," "Fourfold," or "Sixfold" knots and are used to prevent a rope from passing through a ring or block as well as for shortening. All gradations from the double to the sixfold are shown in Fig. 69, both in process of making and as they appear when drawn taut. Another very simple form of shortening is shown in Fig. 70 and is known as

FIG. 67.—Twofold shortening (making).   FIG. 68.—Twofold shortening (taut).

the "Single Plait," or "Chain Knot." To make this shortening, make a running loop (*A*, Fig. 70), then draw a bight of the rope through this loop, as shown at *B*, draw another bight through this, as at *C* to *D*, and

FIG. 69.—Three- and fivefold shortening.

continue in this way until the rope is shortened to the desired length; the free end should then be fastened by passing a bit of stick through the last loop, *F*, or by running the free end through the last loop, as at *E*. To undo this shortening, it is only necessary to slip out the free end, or the bit of wood, and pull on the end, when

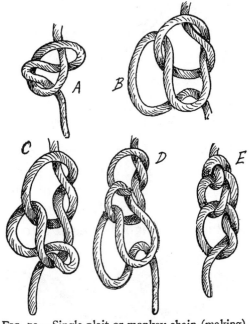

FIG. 70.—Single plait or monkey chain (making).

the entire knot will quickly unravel. The "Twist," or "Double Chain," is made in a similar manner but is commenced in a different way (*A*, Fig. 71). It may also be made with three separate pieces of line, as shown in *B*, Fig. 71. Hold the double loop in the left hand; the part *A* is then brought over *B*; with a half turn *B* is crossed over to *A*, and then proceed as in the ordinary three-strand plait until the end of loop is reached,

FIG. 70 *F.*—Monkey chain or single plait (complete).

when the loose end is fastened by passing through the bight and the completed shortening appears as in Fig. 72. This same process is often used by Mexicans and Westerners in making bridles, headstalls, etc., of leather. The leather to be used is slit lengthwise from near one end to near the other, as shown in Fig. 73, and the braid is formed as described. The result appears

as in Fig. 74, and in this way the ends of the
leather strap remain uncut, and thus much
stronger and neater than they would be
were three separate strips used.

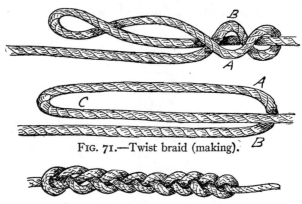

FIG. 71.—Twist braid (making).

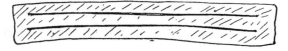

FIG. 72.—Twist braid (complete).

Another handsome knot for shortening is
the more highly ornamental "Open Chain"
(Fig. 75).   Make the first loop of the rope

FIG. 73.—Leather cut to braid.

secure by a twist of the rope and then pass
the loose end through the preceding loop,
to right and left alternately, until the knot
is complete.

The simplest of all shortenings consists of a loop taken in the rope with the bights

Fig. 74.—Leather braid (complete).

seized to the standing part (Fig. 76). This is particularly well adapted to heavy rope

Fig. 75.—Open chain.

or where a shortening must be made quickly. Fig. 77 shows another very simple shorten-

Fig. 76.—Seized shortening.

ing, which requires no description. This will not withstand a very great strain but is secure from untying by accident and is very useful for taking up spare rope of lashings on bundles or baggage. "Sheepshanks,"

FIG. 77.—Bow shortening.

or "Dogshanks," are widely used for shortening rope, especially where both ends are fast, as they can be readily made in the

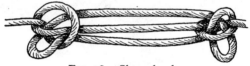

FIG. 78.—Sheepshank.

centre of a tied rope. There are several forms of these useful knots. The best and most secure form is shown in Fig. 78. A

FIG. 79.—Another sheepshank.

simple running knot is first made; a bend is pushed through the loop, which is then drawn taut; the other end of the bend is

fastened in a similar manner and the shortening is complete   A much simpler form is
shown in Fig. 79, but this can hardly be
depended upon unless the ends are seized,

FIG. 80.—Sheepshank with ends seized.

as shown in Fig. 80.   Figs. 81–82 illustrate
two other forms of shortenings, but these
can only be used where the end of the rope

FIG. 81.—Sheepshank for free-ended rope.

is free, and are intended for more permanent
fastenings than the ordinary sheepshank;
while Fig. 83 is particularly adapted to be

FIG. 82.—Sheepshank for free-ended rope.

cast loose at a moment's notice by jerking
out the toggles, A, B.

Grommets are round, endless rings of
rope useful in a myriad ways aboard ship

as well as ashore. They are often used as handles for chests, for rings with which to play quoits, to lengthen rope, and in many similar ways. The grommet is formed of a single strand of rope *five times as long as the circumference of the grommet when*

FIG. 83.—Sheepshank with toggle.

complete. Take the strand and lay one end across the other at the size of loop required and with the long end follow the grooves or "lay" of the strand until back to where you started (Fig. 84), thus forming a two-stranded ring. Then continue twisting the free end between the turns already made until the three-strand ring is complete (Fig. 85). Now finish and secure the ends by making overhand knots, pass the ends underneath the nearest strands and trim ends off close (Fig. 86). If care is taken and you remember to keep a strong twist on the strand while "laying up" the grommet, the finished ring will be as

firm and smooth and endless as the original
rope.

A "Sevagee" or "Selvagee" strap is another kind of ring (Fig. 87). This is made
by passing a number of strands or yarns

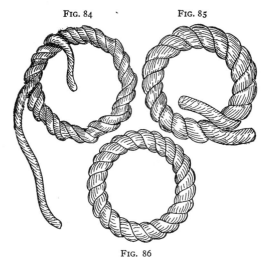

FIG. 84   FIG. 85

FIG. 86
FIGS. 84, 85, and 86.—Grommet complete and making.

around pins or nails set in a board (Fig. 88),
and binding the whole together with a seizing of yarn or marline (Fig. 89). These are
strong, durable straps much used for blocks
aboard ship, for handles to boxes and chests,
and in many similar ways. A "Flemish
Eye" (Fig. 90) is an eye made in a manner

much like that employed in forming the
selvagee strap.   Take a spar or piece of
wood the size of the intended eye *A*.

FIG. 87.—Selvagee strap.

Around this wood lay a number of pieces
of yarn or marline, *B, B, B,* and fasten them
by tying with twine as at *C*.   Whip the

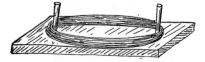

FIG. 88.—Selvagee board.

FIG. 89.—Seizing a selvagee strap.

piece of rope in which eye is to be formed
and unravel and open out the strands as
at *D*.   Lap the yarns over the wood and

the stops *B*, and fasten together by over-hand knots *E*, worm the free ends under and over and then bring up the ends of the stops *B* and tie around the strands of eye as shown. The eye may be finished neatly by

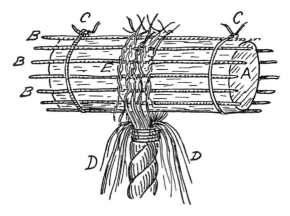

FIG. 90 *A*.—Making Flemish eye.

whipping all around with yarn or marline, and will then appear as in Fig. 90 *B*. An "Artificial Eye" (Fig. 91) is still another form of eye which will be found useful and in some ways easier and quicker to make than a spliced eye, besides being stronger.

Take the end of a rope and unlay one strand; place the two remaining strands back alongside of the standing part (Fig. 92).

Pass the loose strand which has been unlaid over the end, and follow around the spaces between the two strands and then around eye,—as in making a grommet,—until it

FIG. 90 *B.*—Flemish eye (complete).

FIG. 91.—Artificial eye.

returns down the standing part and lies under the eye with the strands (Fig. 93). Then divide the strands, taper them down, and whip the whole with yarn or marline (Fig. 94).

Still another eye which at times will be useful is the "Throat Seizing," shown in Fig. 95. This is made by opening the end slightly and lashing it to the standing part

FIG. 92

FIG. 93
FIGS. 92 and 93.—Making artificial eye.

FIG. 94.—Artificial eye (whipped).

FIG. 95.—Throat seizing.

as shown. Another ring sometimes used is illustrated in Fig. 96, and is easily and quickly made by lashing the two ends of a

Fig. 96.—Lashed cut-splice.

short rope to the standing part of another. Cuckolds' necks with lashings or "Clinches" are also used for the same purpose.

CHAPTER VI

Lashings, Seizings, Splices, etc.

Almost any one can lash a rope more or less satisfactorily, but a knowledge of how to do this properly and in the manner best suited to each case is of great importance to seamen and others having occasion to handle ropes, rigging, or in fact any cordage.

The varieties of lashings, seizings, whippings, and servings are almost innumerable, but a few of the best and most frequently used are the "Wedding Knot" or "Rose Lashing," the "Deadeye Lashing," the "Belaying-pin Splice," the "Necklace Tie," the "Close Band," and "End Pointings." The rose lashing (Fig. 97) is used to join two eyes or ropes finished with loops. The deadeye lashing (Fig. 98) is frequently used on ships' standing rigging and is a familiar sight to every one who has seen a sailing-vessel. It consists of a small line reeved back and forth through the holes in the "deadeyes," *A*; the ends are then seized

to the standing rigging to prevent slipping.   This lashing admits of easy and
rapid lengthening or shortening of the rig-

FIG. 97.—Rose lashing.

ging and is particularly useful in connection
with wire cable.   A similar method may be
used with loops instead of deadeyes (Fig.

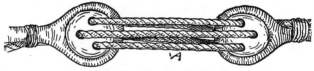

FIG. 98.—Deadeye lashing.

99).   The belaying-pin splice, shown in Fig.
100, is a quick and handy way of fastening two ropes together and is of great value

FIG. 99.—Loop lashing.

when rigging is carried away and some
quick method of joining the severed ends is
required.   Pass a belaying-pin or similar

toggle through an eye or loop in one end
of a rope and pass this through a loop or
eye in the broken rope end. Form a loop
in the other broken end, slip the free end of

FIG. 100.—Belaying-pin splice.

the lanyard through this and around another
toggle or pin and haul taut; then fasten by
half-hitches around standing part (*A*, Fig.
100), or by seizing (*B*, Fig. 100). This is
a strong, reliable fastening and can be tightened up or instantly thrown off at will.

FIG. 101.—Necklace tie.

The necklace tie is useful in holding two
ropes, hawsers, or timbers side by side (Fig.
101). The lashing is passed around and
around the two objects to be joined and the

ends secured by a square knot passed around the band lengthwise. The close band is used for the same purposes as the last and is made in the same manner, but the ends are fastened by drawing through beneath the turns (Fig. 102).

End pointings are very useful as well as ornamental, for while an ordinary seizing or whipping will prevent the strands from

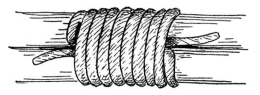

FIG. 102.—Close band.

unravelling, the ends are broad and clumsy and oftentimes are too large to pass through a block or eye large enough for the rest of the rope. The ordinary way of pointing a rope is to first whip as described (Fig. 4), and then unlay the end as for the Flemish eye. Take out about two-thirds of the yarns and twist each in two. Take two parts of different yarns and twist together with finger and thumb, keeping the lay on the yarn and thus forming left-handed stuff known as "nettles." Comb out the rest of the yarn with a knife, leaving a few to lay back upon the rope. Now pass three turns of twine like a timber-hitch tightly around the part where the nettles separate and fasten the twine, and while passing

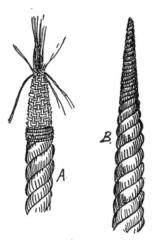

Fig. 103.—Pointing a rope.

this "warp" lay the nettles backward and forward with each turn. The ends are now whipped with twine or yarn and finally "snaked," which is done by taking the end under and over the outer turns of the seizing alternately. If the rope is small a stick is often put in the upper part to strengthen it or the tip may be finished with a small eye. If properly done a pointed rope is very handsome and appears as in *B*, Fig. 103. Another simple way of finish-

FIG. 104.—Ending rope.

FIG. 105.—Ending rope.

ing a rope end is to seize the end, as at *A*, Fig. 104, and open out the strands, bring the strands back alongside the rope, and whip the whole (Fig. 105).

Splicing is, in many cases, more useful and better than tying or bending ropes together and a good splice always looks neater and more ship-shape than a knot, no matter how well-made it may be. A person familiar with splicing will turn in a splice almost as quickly as the ordinary man can tie a secure knot, and in many cases, where the rope must pass through sheaves or

blocks, a splice is absolutely necessary to
fasten two ropes or two parts of a parted
rope together. The simplest of all splices

FIG. 106.—Short splice.

is known as the "Short Splice" (Fig. 106).
This is made as follows: Untwist the ends
of the rope for a few inches and seize with

FIG. 106 *D.*—Short splice (continued).

twine to prevent further unwinding, as
shown at *A*, *A;* also seize the end of each
strand to prevent unravelling and grease

or wax the strands until smooth and even.
Now place the two ends of the ropes together as shown at B, B. Then with a
marline-spike, or a pointed stick, work open
the strand 1 c, and through this pass the
strand A of the other rope; then open
strand 2 and pass the next strand of the
other rope through it and then the same
way with the third strand. Next open up
the strands of the other rope, below the
seizing, and pass the strands of the first rope
through as before, 3 A, B. The ropes will
now appear as in Fig. 106, D. Now untwist
the six strands and cut away about half the
yarns from each and seize the ends as before;
pass these reduced strands through under
the whole strands of the rope—the strands
of the left under the strands of the right
rope and *vice versa*—for two or three lays
and then cut off projecting ends, after
drawing all as tight as you can. If an
extra-neat splice is desired the strands
should be gradually tapered as you proceed,
and in this way a splice but little larger than
the original diameter of the rope will result.
The only difficulty you will find in making
this splice is in getting the strands to come

together in such a way that two strands will not run under the same strand of the opposite rope. To avoid this, bear in mind that the *first strand must be passed over the strand which is first next to it and through under the second and out between the second and third.* In the following operations the strands are passed *over* the third and *under*

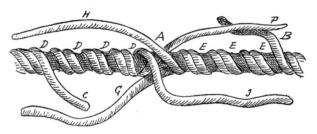

FIG. 107.—Long splice.

the fourth; but the figures will make this perfectly clear. A far better and stronger splice is the "Long Splice," which will run through any block or tackle which will admit the rope itself; indeed, a well-made long splice cannot be distinguished from the rope itself after a few days' use (Fig. 107). To make this useful splice, unlay the ends of the rope about four times 'as much as for the short splice, or from four to five feet, unlay one strand in each rope for half as

much again; place the middle strands
together as at *A*, then the additional strands
will appear as at *B* and *C*, and the spiral
groove, left where they were unlaid, will
appear as at *D* and *E*. Take off the two
central strands, *F* and *G*, and lay them into

FIG. 108.—Eye splice.

the grooves, *D*, *E*, until they meet *B* and *C*,
and be sure and keep them tightly twisted
while so doing. Then take strands *H* and *J*,
cut out half the yarns in each, make an overhand knot in them and tuck the ends under
the next lays as in a short splice. Do the
same with strands *B*, *C* and *F*, *G*; dividing,
knotting, and sticking the divided strands in
the same way. Finally stretch the rope

tight, pull and pound and roll the splice until smooth and round, and trim off all loose ends close to the rope.

An "Eye Splice" (Fig. 108) is very easy to make and is useful and handy in a great variety of ways. It is made in the same manner as the short splice, but instead of splicing the two ends together, the end of

FIG. 109.—Cut splice.

the rope is unlaid and then bent around and spliced into its own strands of the standing part, as shown in the illustration. A "Cut Splice" (Fig. 109) is made just as an eye splice or short splice, but instead of splicing two ropes together end to end, or splicing an end into a standing part, the ends are lapped and each is spliced into the standing part of the other, thus forming a loop or eye in the centre of a rope. Once the short and long splices are mastered, all other splices, as well as many useful variations, will come easy. Oftentimes, for example, one strand of a rope may become worn, frayed, or broken, while the remaining strands are perfectly sound. In such cases the weak strand may be unlaid and cut off and then a new strand of the same length is laid up in the groove left by the old strand exactly as in a long splice; the ends are then tapered, stuck under the lay, as in a short splice, and the repair is complete; and if well done will never show and will be as strong as the original rope.

CHAPTER VII

Fancy Knots and Rope Work

The knots and splices described above are all more for practical use than ornament, although such shortenings as the Single and Double plaits, the Chain knots, the Twofold, Fourfold, and Sixfold knots, and others are often used for ornamental purposes only. A certain class of knots are, however, really ornamental and seldom serve to fasten two ropes together, or to make any object fast to another. They are, however, very useful in many ways, especially aboard ship, and they are so handsome and interesting that every one interested in rope work should learn to make them. The simplest of the fancy knots is known as the "Single Crown" (Fig. 110). To form this knot unlay the strands of a new, flexible rope for six to eight inches and whip the ends of each strand, as well as the standing part, to prevent further untwisting. Hold the rope in your left hand and fold one strand over

and away from you, as shown in *A*, Fig. 111.
Then fold the next strand over *A* (see *B*,
Fig. 111), and then, while holding these in
place with thumb and finger, pass the strand
C over strand *B*, and through the bight of
A as shown in the illustration.   Now pull

FIG. 110.—Single crown.   FIG. 111.—Single crown (making).

all ends tight and work the bights up smooth
and snug; cut off ends and the knot is
complete.   This single crown is a very poor
knot to stand by itself, however, and is
mainly valuable as a basis for other more
complicated knots and for ending up rope.
To end up a rope with a crown it is merely
necessary to leave the projecting ends long
and then by bringing them down tuck under
the strands of the standing part, as shown in
Fig. 112.   Then halve the strands and tuck

again, as in making a short splice, until the result appears as in Fig. 113. This makes a neat, handy, and ship-shape finish to a

FIG. 112.—Single crown tucked (making).

FIG. 113.—Single crown tucked (complete).

rope's end and is very useful for painters, halyards, etc. It will never work loose like a seizing and is quickly put on at any time,

FIG. 114.—Wall knot.

whereas to make a seizing one must be provided with small stuff of some sort, and this is frequently not at hand. The "Wall Knot" (Fig. 114) is almost as simple as the crown, and in fact is practically a

crown reversed.   In making this knot bring
C downward and across the standing part;
then bring A over C and around standing
part and finally bring B over A and up
through bight of C, Fig. 115.   When drawn
snug the ends may be trimmed off close

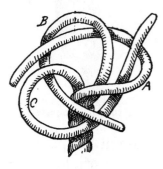

FIG. 115.—Wall knot
(making).

FIG. 116.—Wall knot
(tucked).

or they may be tucked and tapered as in
the crown and will then appear as in Fig.
116.   As in the case of the crown knot, the
wall is mainly of value as an ending when
ends are tucked, or as a basis for more
ornamental knots such as the "Wall and
Crown," or "Double Wall," or "Double
Crown."   It is also very largely used in making "Shroud Knots" (Fig. 117).   The common shroud knot is made by opening up the

strands of a rope's end as for a short splice and placing the two ends together in the same way. Then single "wall" the strands of one rope around the standing part of another against the lay, taper the ends, and

FIG. 117.—Shroud knot
(complete).

FIG. 118.—Shroud knot
(making).

tuck and serve all with yarn or marline (Fig. 118). The "French Shroud Knot" is far neater and better, but is a little harder to make. Open up the strands and place closely together as for the short splice; make a loop of strand *A*, pass the end of *B* through the bight of *A*, as at *C*, make a loop of strand *D*, and pass the end of strand *A* through it as at *D;* then pass the end of

strand *D* through the bight of strand *B* and
one side is complete.   Repeat the operation
on the other side, draw all ends taut, and

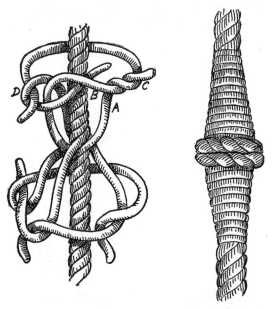

FIG. 119.—French shroud   FIG. 120.—French shroud
knot (making).   knot (complete).

taper and tuck the ends. The whole
should then be served carefully and the
finished knot will appear as in Fig. 120.

Double wall and double crown as well
as the beautiful double wall-and-crown
knots are made exactly like the single

crown or wall but instead of trimming
off or tucking the ends they are carried
around a second time following the lay of

FIG. 121 *A*.—Making double   FIG. 121 *B*.—Making double
        crown.   wall.

the first, as shown in Fig. 121, which shows
the construction of a double crown at *A*,

FIG. 122.—Double crown   FIG. 123.—Double wall
     (complete).   (complete).

and a double wall at *B*. When finished,
the ends may be tucked or trimmed and
the two knots will look like Figs. 122 and 123.

A far better effect is obtained by "Crowning" a wall knot. This is done by first making a single wall knot and then by bringing strand *A* up over the top and laying *B* across *A* and bringing *C* over *B* and through the bight of *A;* a crown knot is formed above the wall, as shown in Figs. 124 and 125. This is the foundation of the

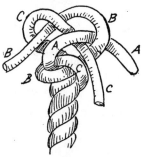

FIG. 124.—Wall crowned (making).

FIG. 125.—Wall crowned (complete).

most beautiful of rope-end knots, known as the "Double Wall and Crown," or "Manrope Knot," illustrated in Fig. 126. Make your single wall and crown it, but leave the strands all slack; then pass the ends up and through the bights of the slack single-wall knot and then push them alongside the strands in the single crown; push-

ing them through the same bight in the
crown and downward through the walling.
This may seem quite difficult, but if you
have learned the wall and crown you will
find it simple enough, for it is really merely
"following" the strands of the single wall
and crown. The result, if properly done,

FIG. 126.—Double wall and   FIG. 127.—Double wall and
          crown.   crown (complete).

and ends drawn tight and cut off closely,
is surprising, and to the uninitiated most
perplexing, for if the ends are tapered and
tucked through the standing part of the
ropes, as shown in Fig. 127, there will be no
sign of a beginning or ending to this knot.
This is probably the most useful of decora-
tive knots and is largely used aboard ship
for finishing the ends of rope railings, the
ends of man-ropes, for the ends of yoke-

lines and to form "stoppers" or "toggles"
to bucket handles, slings, etc. Its use in
this way is illustrated in Figs. 128–130,
which show how to make a handy topsail-
halyard toggle from an eye splice turned
in a short piece of rope and finished with a
double wall and crown at the end. These
toggles are very useful about small boats,
as they may be used as stops for furling

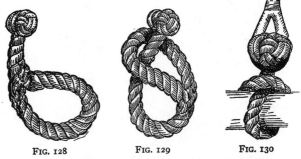

FIG. 128   FIG. 129   FIG. 130

FIGS. 128, 129, and 130.—Topsail-halyard toggle.

sails, for slings around gaffs or spars, for
hoisting, and in a variety of other ways
which will at once suggest themselves to
the boating man.

The most difficult of ending knots and
one which you should certainly learn is the
"Matthew Walker" (Fig. 131), also known
as the "Stopper Knot." To form this

splendid knot, pass one strand around the
standing part of the rope and through its

FIG. 131.—Matthew Walker (making)

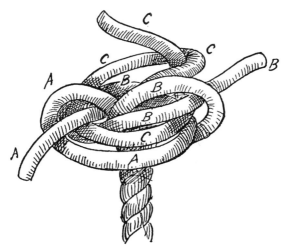

FIG. 132.—Matthew Walker (complete but slack).

own bight, then pass *B* underneath and
through bight of *A*, and through its own

bight also; next pass *C* underneath and
around and through the bights of *A*, *B*,
and its own bight. The knot will now
appear as in Fig. 132, but by carefully haul-
ing the ends around and working the bight
taut a little at a time the knot will assume
the appearance shown in Fig. 133. This
is a handsome and useful knot and is widely

FIG. 133.—Matthew Walker (complete).

used on ends of ropes where they pass
through holes, as for bucket handles, ropes
for trap-door handles, chest handles, etc.
The knot is well adapted for such purposes,
as it is hard, close, and presents an almost
flat shoulder on its lower side.

The "Turk's Head," Figs. 135 and 136,
is a knot much used aboard yachts and war-
ships and is so handsome and ornamental
that it is a great favorite. It is used in

ornamenting rigging, in forming shoulders
or rings on stays or ropes to hold other gear
in place, to ornament yoke lines, and for
forming slip-collars on knife lanyards.   It
is also used to form collars around stanchions or spars, and, placed around a rope
close beneath a man-rope knot, it gives a
beautiful finish.   When made of small line
sailors often use the Turk's Head as a neck-
erchief fastener.   Although so elaborate in
effect, it is really an easy knot to make, and
while you may have difficulty in getting it
right at first a little patience and practice
will enable you to become proficient and
capable of tying it rapidly and easily in any
place or position.   To make a Turk's Head,
have a smooth, round stick, or other object,
and some closely twisted or braided small
line.   Pass two turns of the line around the
rod, A, Fig. 135, from left to right, and pass
the upper bight down through the lower
and reeve the upper end down through it, as
at B.   Then pass the bight up again and
run the end over the lower bight and up
between it and the upper bight.   Turn the
upper bight again through the lower one
and pass the end over what is now the upper

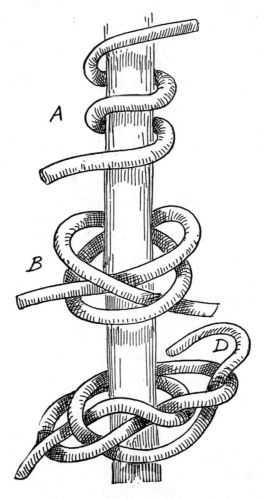

Fig. 135.—Making Turk's head.

bight and between it and the lower, *C*, Fig.
135. Now work from left to right, following the lay of the knot (or, in other words,
passing your long end alongside the first
end), *D*, Fig. 135, until a braid of two or

FIG. 136.—Turks' heads.   FIG. 137.—Turk's cap.

more lays is completed, as shown in Fig. 136.
The Turk's Head may be drawn as tight as
desired around the rope, or rod, by working
up the slack and drawing all bights taut.
A variation of the knot may be formed by
making the first part as described and then

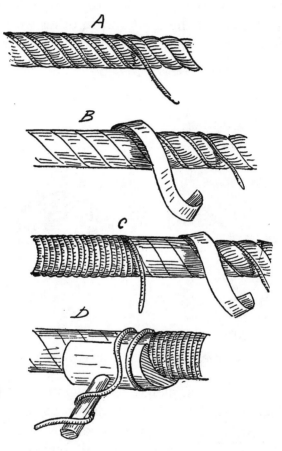

FIG. 138.—Worming, parcelling, and serving.

by slipping the knot to the end of the rod; work one side tighter than the other until the "Head" forms a complete cap, as shown in Fig. 137. This makes a splendid finish for the ends of flagpoles, stanchions, etc.

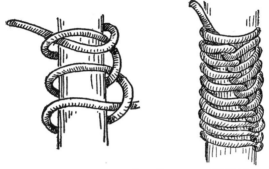

FIG. 139.—Half-hitch work.   FIG. 140.—Half-hitch work.

Ropes that are to be used as hand-lines, stanchions, man-ropes, railings, or in fact wherever a neat appearance counts, are usually wormed, served, and parcelled. Worming consists in twisting a small line into the grooves between the strands of rope, *A*, Fig. 138. This fills up the grooves and makes the rope smooth and ready for serving or parcelling. Parcelling consists in covering the rope already wormed with a strip of canvas wound spirally around it

with the edges overlapping, *B*, Fig. 138.
Serving is merely wrapping the rope with
spun yarn, marline, or other small stuff,
C, Fig. 138. Although this may all be done
by hand, yet it can be accomplished far
better by using a "Serving Mallet," shown
in *D*, Fig. 138. This instrument enables

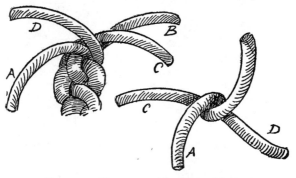

FIG. 141.—Four-strand braid (making).

you to work tighter and more evenly than
by hand, but in either case you must have
the rope, to be served stretched tightly between two uprights. Often a rope is served
without parcelling and for ordinary purposes parcelling is not required. A variation of serving is made by "half-hitch"
work, as shown in Figs. 139–140. This is
very pretty when well done and is very easy

to accomplish. Take a half-hitch around
the rope to be served, then another below it;
draw snug; take another half-hitch and so
on until the object is covered and the series

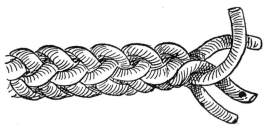

FIG. 142.—Four-strand braid (complete).

of half-hitch knots forms a spiral twist, as
shown in the illustrations. Bottles, jugs,
ropes, stanchions, fenders, and numerous
other articles may be covered with half-
hitch work; and as you become more expert

FIG. 143.—Crown-braid.

you will be able to use several lines of half-
hitches at the same time. Four-strand
braiding is also highly ornamental and is
easy and simple. The process is illustrated

in Fig. 141, and consists in crossing the opposite strands across and past one another, as shown in *A*, *B*, *C*, Fig 141.   Still

FIG. 144.—Rope buckle.

more ornamental is the "Crown-braid" which appears, when finished, as in Fig. 143. The process of forming this braid is exactly

FIG. 145.—Swivels.

like ordinary crowning and does not require any description; it may be done with any number of strands, but four or six are usually as many as the beginner cares to handle at one time.

When the rope-worker has mastered all the knots, ties, bends, hitches, and splices I

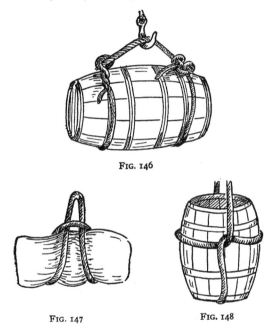

FIG. 146

FIG. 147   FIG. 148

FIGS. 146, 147, and 148.—Slings.

have described, he will find a new field open to the use of rope in innumerable ways. Barrels, casks, bales, or other objects may be roped, or slung, with ease and security; ropes will be pressed into service for straps and belts; and buckles may be readily formed by the simple expedient shown in Fig. 144. If a swivel is required it can be arranged as shown in Fig. 145, while several simple slings are illustrated in Figs. 146–148. In a factory, or machine shop, rope belting will often prove far better than leather, and if well spliced together will run very smoothly and evenly even on long stretches. As a recreation for killing time aboard ship, or on rainy vacation days, few occupations will prove more enjoyable than tying fancy knots and making new splices and bends or inventing new variations of the numerous hitches, ties, and knots you already know.

Halters for Animals

Every now and then a temporary halter is needed for a horse, and in Fig. 149 such a halter is shown. This halter is made by putting the end of a long rope around the neck of the horse and then tying a common bow-line knot. (See Fig. 150.) Fig. 151 shows the second step to be followed, that of passing the rope around the animal's head twice, while Fig. 152 shows how

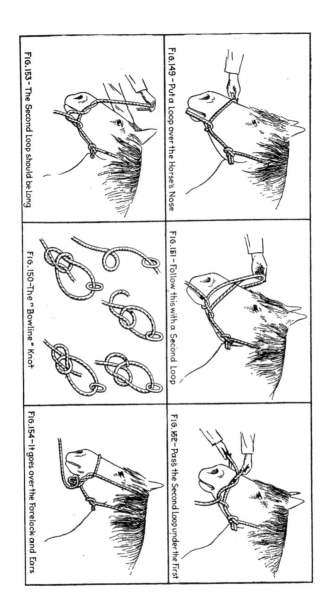

FIG. 149 – Put a Loop over the Horse's Nose

FIG. 151 – Follow this with a Second Loop

FIG. 152 – Pass the Second Loop under the First

FIG. 153 – The Second Loop should be long

FIG. 150 – The " Bowline " Knot

FIG. 154 – It goes over the Forelock and Ears

the second loop is passed under the first. In Fig. 153 the rope is shown sufficiently long enough to enable it to be passed over the ears of the animal and leave the halter completed, as shown in Fig. 154.

INDEX

A CATALOG OF SELECTED
DOVER BOOKS
IN ALL FIELDS OF INTEREST

A CATALOG OF SELECTED DOVER
BOOKS IN ALL FIELDS OF INTEREST

CONCERNING THE SPIRITUAL IN ART, Wassily Kandinsky. Pioneering work by father of abstract art. Thoughts on color theory, nature of art. Analysis of earlier masters. 12 illustrations. 80pp. of text. 5⅜ x 8½. 0-486-23411-8

CELTIC ART: The Methods of Construction, George Bain. Simple geometric techniques for making Celtic interlacements, spirals, Kells-type initials, animals, humans, etc. Over 500 illustrations. 160pp. 9 x 12. (Available in U.S. only.) 0-486-22923-8

AN ATLAS OF ANATOMY FOR ARTISTS, Fritz Schider. Most thorough reference work on art anatomy in the world. Hundreds of illustrations, including selections from works by Vesalius, Leonardo, Goya, Ingres, Michelangelo, others. 593 illustrations. 192pp. 7⅛ x 10¼. 0-486-20241-0

CELTIC HAND STROKE-BY-STROKE (Irish Half-Uncial from "The Book of Kells"): An Arthur Baker Calligraphy Manual, Arthur Baker. Complete guide to creating each letter of the alphabet in distinctive Celtic manner. Covers hand position, strokes, pens, inks, paper, more. Illustrated. 48pp. 8¼ x 11. 0-486-24336-2

EASY ORIGAMI, John Montroll. Charming collection of 32 projects (hat, cup, pelican, piano, swan, many more) specially designed for the novice origami hobbyist. Clearly illustrated easy-to-follow instructions insure that even beginning papercrafters will achieve successful results. 48pp. 8¼ x 11. 0-486-27298-2

BLOOMINGDALE'S ILLUSTRATED 1886 CATALOG: Fashions, Dry Goods and Housewares, Bloomingdale Brothers. Famed merchants' extremely rare catalog depicting about 1,700 products: clothing, housewares, firearms, dry goods, jewelry, more. Invaluable for dating, identifying vintage items. Also, copyright-free graphics for artists, designers. Co-published with Henry Ford Museum & Greenfield Village. 160pp. 8¼ x 11. 0-486-25780-0

THE ART OF WORLDLY WISDOM, Baltasar Gracian. "Think with the few and speak with the many," "Friends are a second existence," and "Be able to forget" are among this 1637 volume's 300 pithy maxims. A perfect source of mental and spiritual refreshment, it can be opened at random and appreciated either in brief or at length. 128pp. 5⅜ x 8½. 0-486-44034-6

JOHNSON'S DICTIONARY: A Modern Selection, Samuel Johnson (E. L. McAdam and George Milne, eds.). This modern version reduces the original 1755 edition's 2,300 pages of definitions and literary examples to a more manageable length, retaining the verbal pleasure and historical curiosity of the original. 480pp. 5³⁄₁₆ x 8¼. 0-486-44089-3

ADVENTURES OF HUCKLEBERRY FINN, Mark Twain, Illustrated by E. W. Kemble. A work of eternal richness and complexity, a source of ongoing critical debate, and a literary landmark, Twain's 1885 masterpiece about a barefoot boy's journey of self-discovery has enthralled readers around the world. This handsome clothbound reproduction of the first edition features all 174 of the original black-and-white illustrations. 368pp. 5⅜ x 8½. 0-486-44322-1

STICKLEY CRAFTSMAN FURNITURE CATALOGS, Gustav Stickley and L. & J. G. Stickley. Beautiful, functional furniture in two authentic catalogs from 1910. 594 illustrations, including 277 photos, show settles, rockers, armchairs, reclining chairs, bookcases, desks, tables. 183pp. 6½ x 9¼.   0-486-23838-5

AMERICAN LOCOMOTIVES IN HISTORIC PHOTOGRAPHS: 1858 to 1949, Ron Ziel (ed.). A rare collection of 126 meticulously detailed official photographs, called "builder portraits," of American locomotives that majestically chronicle the rise of steam locomotive power in America. Introduction. Detailed captions. xi+ 129pp. 9 x 12.   0-486-27393-8

AMERICA'S LIGHTHOUSES: An Illustrated History, Francis Ross Holland, Jr. Delightfully written, profusely illustrated fact-filled survey of over 200 American light-houses since 1716. History, anecdotes, technological advances, more. 240pp. 8 x 10¾.
0-486-25576-X

TOWARDS A NEW ARCHITECTURE, Le Corbusier. Pioneering manifesto by founder of "International School." Technical and aesthetic theories, views of industry, eco-nomics, relation of form to function, "mass-production split" and much more. Profusely illustrated. 320pp. 6⅛ x 9¼. (Available in U.S. only.)   0-486-25023-7

HOW THE OTHER HALF LIVES, Jacob Riis. Famous journalistic record, expos-ing poverty and degradation of New York slums around 1900, by major social reformer. 100 striking and influential photographs. 233pp. 10 x 7⅞.   0-486-22012-5

FRUIT KEY AND TWIG KEY TO TREES AND SHRUBS, William M. Harlow. One of the handiest and most widely used identification aids. Fruit key covers 120 deciduous and evergreen species; twig key 160 deciduous species. Easily used. Over 300 photographs. 126pp. 5⅜ x 8½.   0-486-20511-8

COMMON BIRD SONGS, Dr. Donald J. Borror. Songs of 60 most common U.S. birds: robins, sparrows, cardinals, bluejays, finches, more–arranged in order of increasing complexity. Up to 9 variations of songs of each species.
Cassette and manual 0-486-99911-4

ORCHIDS AS HOUSE PLANTS, Rebecca Tyson Northen. Grow cattleyas and many other kinds of orchids–in a window, in a case, or under artificial light. 63 illus-trations. 148pp. 5⅜ x 8½.   0-486-23261-1

MONSTER MAZES, Dave Phillips. Masterful mazes at four levels of difficulty. Avoid deadly perils and evil creatures to find magical treasures. Solutions for all 32 exciting illustrated puzzles. 48pp. 8¼ x 11.   0-486-26005-4

MOZART'S DON GIOVANNI (DOVER OPERA LIBRETTO SERIES), Wolfgang Amadeus Mozart. Introduced and translated by Ellen H. Bleiler. Standard Italian libretto, with complete English translation. Convenient and thoroughly portable–an ideal companion for reading along with a recording or the performance itself. Introduction. List of characters. Plot summary. 121pp. 5¼ x 8½. 0-486-24944-1

FRANK LLOYD WRIGHT'S DANA HOUSE, Donald Hoffmann. Pictorial essay of residential masterpiece with over 160 interior and exterior photos, plans, eleva-tions, sketches and studies. 128pp. 9¼ x 10¾.   0-486-29120-0

THE CLARINET AND CLARINET PLAYING, David Pino. Lively, comprehensive work features suggestions about technique, musicianship, and musical interpretation, as well as guidelines for teaching, making your own reeds, and preparing for public performance. Includes an intriguing look at clarinet history. "A godsend," *The Clarinet,* Journal of the International Clarinet Society. Appendixes. 7 illus. 320pp. $5\frac{3}{8}$ x $8\frac{1}{2}$. 0-486-40270-3

HOLLYWOOD GLAMOR PORTRAITS, John Kobal (ed.). 145 photos from 1926-49. Harlow, Gable, Bogart, Bacall; 94 stars in all. Full background on photographers, technical aspects. 160pp. $8\frac{3}{8}$ x $11\frac{1}{4}$. 0-486-23352-9

THE RAVEN AND OTHER FAVORITE POEMS, Edgar Allan Poe. Over 40 of the author's most memorable poems: "The Bells," "Ulalume," "Israfel," "To Helen," "The Conqueror Worm," "Eldorado," "Annabel Lee," many more. Alphabetic lists of titles and first lines. 64pp. $5\frac{3}{16}$ x $8\frac{1}{4}$. 0-486-26685-0

PERSONAL MEMOIRS OF U. S. GRANT, Ulysses Simpson Grant. Intelligent, deeply moving firsthand account of Civil War campaigns, considered by many the finest military memoirs ever written. Includes letters, historic photographs, maps and more. 528pp. $6\frac{1}{8}$ x $9\frac{1}{4}$. 0-486-28587-1

ANCIENT EGYPTIAN MATERIALS AND INDUSTRIES, A. Lucas and J. Harris. Fascinating, comprehensive, thoroughly documented text describes this ancient civilization's vast resources and the processes that incorporated them in daily life, including the use of animal products, building materials, cosmetics, perfumes and incense, fibers, glazed ware, glass and its manufacture, materials used in the mummification process, and much more. 544pp. $6^1/_8$ x $9^1/_4$. (Available in U.S. only.) 0-486-40446-3

RUSSIAN STORIES/RUSSKIE RASSKAZY: A Dual-Language Book, edited by Gleb Struve. Twelve tales by such masters as Chekhov, Tolstoy, Dostoevsky, Pushkin, others. Excellent word-for-word English translations on facing pages, plus teaching and study aids, Russian/English vocabulary, biographical/critical introductions, more. 416pp. $5\frac{3}{8}$ x $8\frac{1}{2}$. 0-486-26244-8

PHILADELPHIA THEN AND NOW: 60 Sites Photographed in the Past and Present, Kenneth Finkel and Susan Oyama. Rare photographs of City Hall, Logan Square, Independence Hall, Betsy Ross House, other landmarks juxtaposed with contemporary views. Captures changing face of historic city. Introduction. Captions. 128pp. $8\frac{1}{4}$ x 11. 0-486-25790-8

NORTH AMERICAN INDIAN LIFE: Customs and Traditions of 23 Tribes, Elsie Clews Parsons (ed.). 27 fictionalized essays by noted anthropologists examine religion, customs, government, additional facets of life among the Winnebago, Crow, Zuni, Eskimo, other tribes. 480pp. $6\frac{1}{8}$ x $9\frac{1}{4}$. 0-486-27377-6

TECHNICAL MANUAL AND DICTIONARY OF CLASSICAL BALLET, Gail Grant. Defines, explains, comments on steps, movements, poses and concepts. 15-page pictorial section. Basic book for student, viewer. 127pp. $5\frac{3}{8}$ x $8\frac{1}{2}$. 0-486-21843-0

THE MALE AND FEMALE FIGURE IN MOTION: 60 Classic Photographic Sequences, Eadweard Muybridge. 60 true-action photographs of men and women walking, running, climbing, bending, turning, etc., reproduced from rare 19th-century masterpiece. vi + 121pp. 9 x 12. 0-486-24745-7

CATALOG OF DOVER BOOKS

LIGHT AND SHADE: A Classic Approach to Three-Dimensional Drawing, Mrs. Mary P. Merrifield. Handy reference clearly demonstrates principles of light and shade by revealing effects of common daylight, sunshine, and candle or artificial light on geometrical solids. 13 plates. 64pp. 5⅜ x 8½. 0-486-44143-1

ASTROLOGY AND ASTRONOMY: A Pictorial Archive of Signs and Symbols, Ernst and Johanna Lehner. Treasure trove of stories, lore, and myth, accompanied by more than 300 rare illustrations of planets, the Milky Way, signs of the zodiac, comets, meteors, and other astronomical phenomena. 192pp. 8⅜ x 11. 0-486-43981-X

JEWELRY MAKING: Techniques for Metal, Tim McCreight. Easy-to-follow instructions and carefully executed illustrations describe tools and techniques, use of gems and enamels, wire inlay, casting, and other topics. 72 line illustrations and diagrams. 176pp. 8¼ x 10⅞. 0-486-44043-5

MAKING BIRDHOUSES: Easy and Advanced Projects, Gladstone Califf. Easy-to-follow instructions include diagrams for everything from a one-room house for bluebirds to a forty-two-room structure for purple martins. 56 plates; 4 figures. 80pp. 8¾ x 6⅜. 0-486-44183-0

LITTLE BOOK OF LOG CABINS: How to Build and Furnish Them, William S. Wicks. Handy how-to manual, with instructions and illustrations for building cabins in the Adirondack style, fireplaces, stairways, furniture, beamed ceilings, and more. 102 line drawings. 96pp. 8¾ x 6⅜. 0-486-44259-4

THE SEASONS OF AMERICA PAST, Eric Sloane. From "sugaring time" and strawberry picking to Indian summer and fall harvest, a whole year's activities described in charming prose and enhanced with 79 of the author's own illustrations. 160pp. 8¼ x 11. 0-486-44220-9

THE METROPOLIS OF TOMORROW, Hugh Ferriss. Generous, prophetic vision of the metropolis of the future, as perceived in 1929. Powerful illustrations of towering structures, wide avenues, and rooftop parks–all features in many of today's modern cities. 59 illustrations. 144pp. 8¼ x 11. 0-486-43727-2

THE PATH TO ROME, Hilaire Belloc. This 1902 memoir abounds in lively vignettes from a vanished time, recounting a pilgrimage on foot across the Alps and Apennines in order to "see all Europe which the Christian Faith has saved." 77 of the author's original line drawings complement his sparkling prose. 272pp. 5⅜ x 8½. 0-486-44001-X

THE HISTORY OF RASSELAS: Prince of Abissinia, Samuel Johnson. Distinguished English writer attacks eighteenth-century optimism and man's unrealistic estimates of what life has to offer. 112pp. 5⅜ x 8½. 0-486-44094-X

A VOYAGE TO ARCTURUS, David Lindsay. A brilliant flight of pure fancy, where wild creatures crowd the fantastic landscape and demented torturers dominate victims with their bizarre mental powers. 272pp. 5⅜ x 8½. 0-486-44198-9

Paperbound unless otherwise indicated. Available at your book dealer, online at **www.doverpublications.com**, or by writing to Dept. GI, Dover Publications, Inc., 31 East 2nd Street, Mineola, NY 11501. For current price information or for free catalogs (please indicate field of interest), write to Dover Publications or log on to **www.doverpublications.com** and see every Dover book in print. Dover publishes more than 500 books each year on science, elementary and advanced mathematics, biology, music, art, literary history, social sciences, and other areas.